HOW TO START YOUR OWN PROFITABLE BUSINESS

Easy Beginner's Guide to Understanding Small Business Basics, Maintaining Momentum and Fulfilling your Entrepreneurial Dream

I0427011

Renee H. Thomas

TABLE OF CONTENTS

Introduction

01 Introduction to Entrepreneurship

02 Plan Your Business

03 Executing Your Business Idea

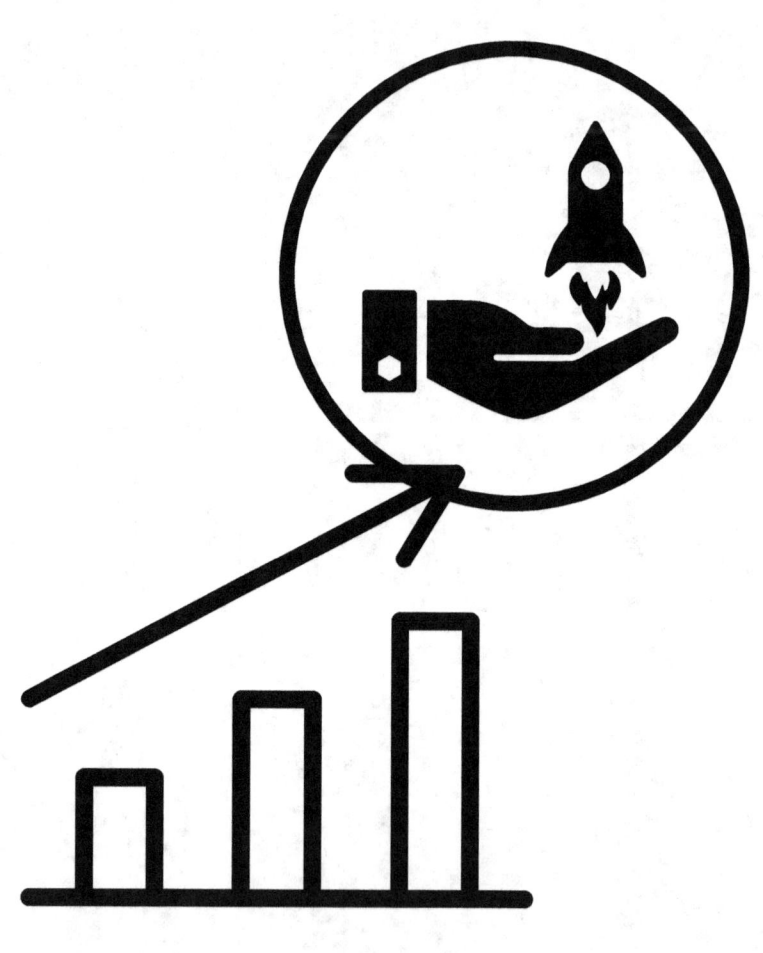

INTRODUCTION

In a world full with options, the prospect of launching your own lucrative business has never been more appealing—or terrifying. Many prospective entrepreneurs are drawn to the promise of freedom, creativity, and financial success, but the route to establishing a successful business is fraught with hurdles and uncertainty. Whether you're driven by a revolutionary idea, a burning passion, or an insatiable yearning for autonomy, the road from concept to profit is an exciting experience that requires perseverance, tenacity, and strategic vision.

From Idea to Profit is your compass for navigating the maze of entrepreneurship. This book, which draws on decades of accumulated expertise from seasoned company executives, creative startups, and entrepreneurial gurus, is a road map for making your ambitions come true. It's more than just beginning a firm; it's about building the framework for long-term success, sustainability, and expansion.

From developing a compelling company concept to implementing a strong strategy, each chapter is designed to provide you with the information, skills, and insights you need to survive in today's competitive business world.

But make no mistake: this is not a story about sudden success or get-rich-quick methods. Building a prosperous business needs patience, dedication, and a willingness to view failure as a stepping stone to success. Along the process, you will face failures and times of uncertainty. However, it is precisely in these moments that your character will be shaped and your resolve tested.

From Idea to Profit is more than simply a handbook; it's a companion on the entrepreneurial journey, providing inspiration, insight, and encouragement when the path ahead appears uncertain. Whether you're a seasoned entrepreneur looking for new perspectives or a young visionary just starting out in company, this book is a reliable partner in your quest for success.

So, my reader, are you ready for the experience of a lifetime? Are you ready to realize your full potential, beat the odds, and carve out a position in the history of entrepreneurship? If yes, turn the page and let the trip begin. Your destiny awaits you, and the world is waiting for your light to shine.

CHAPTER ONE
Introduction to Entrepreneurship

Introduction to Entrepreneurship teaches the core ideas and attitude necessary to establish and maintain a successful business. Here are some essential components of Introduction to Entrepreneurship:

- Understanding the Entrepreneurial Mindset: Entrepreneurship begins with a specific mindset— an drive to create, a willingness to take risks, and a desire for progress. It entails spotting possibilities where others perceive barriers and accepting failure as a catalyst for learning and growth.
- Identifying Opportunities for Business Venture: Successful entrepreneurs are adept at identifying market gaps or unmet customer wants. Introduction to Entrepreneurship focuses on improving your ability to identify feasible business prospects and estimate their likelihood of success.
- Assessing Market Demand and Viability: Conducting market research to better understand client demands, tastes, and behaviors is an important element of entrepreneurship. This entails assessing market trends, researching rivals, and determining your target audience to guarantee that your company concept is both viable and popular.

- Developing Problem-Solving Skills: Entrepreneurship frequently demands overcoming obstacles and devising innovative solutions to complicated issues. Introduction to Entrepreneurship encourages you to think critically, adapt to changing conditions, and overcome challenges with tenacity and perseverance.
- Developing Networks and Relationships: Entrepreneurs thrive on cooperation and networking. Introduction to Entrepreneurship highlights the value of developing strong relationships with mentors, investors, suppliers, and consumers to help your firm grow and succeed.
- Embracing Innovation and adaptation: In today's quickly changing corporate scene, adaptation and innovation are critical for keeping ahead of the curve. Introduction to Entrepreneurship promotes a culture of invention, experimentation, and continual development to keep your company current and competitive.
- Managing Resources and Risks: Successful entrepreneurship requires excellent resource management and risk minimization. Introduction to Entrepreneurship teaches you how to handle finances, distribute resources properly, and identify and minimize possible risks to ensure your company's long-term success.

By learning these fundamental ideas of entrepreneurship, aspiring business owners may create the foundations for a successful and lasting firm. Whether you're starting a tech company, a small firm, or a social initiative, Introduction to Entrepreneurship will provide you the information and skills you need to make your entrepreneurial ambitions come true.

Understanding the Entrepreneur's Mindset

Understanding the entrepreneurial attitude is essential for everyone who wants to establish and run a successful business. Here are some strategies to help you cultivate this mindset:

Embrace Creativity and Innovation: Entrepreneurs are creative problem solvers who are continually looking for new ideas and possibilities. Cultivate your creativity by questioning assumptions, thinking outside the box, and investigating novel solutions to issues.

Develop a Growth Mindset: Believe that you can improve your talents and intellect through devotion and hard effort. Instead than viewing failures and setbacks as obstacles, consider them opportunities for learning and progress.

- Take Calculated Risks: Although entrepreneurship requires risk-taking, successful entrepreneurs take calculated risks based on rigorous study and research. Learn how to assess risks and consider possible benefits before making decisions.
- Be Resilient and Persistent: Starting a business is a journey fraught with hurdles and setbacks. Build resilience by recovering from setbacks, being hopeful in the face of adversity, and keeping a long-term perspective.
- Seek chances Everywhere: Teach yourself to see chances for innovation and commercial endeavors in everyday settings. Continue to be interested, analyze industry trends, and listen to client input to find unmet requirements and unexplored markets.
- Be Action-Oriented: Entrepreneurs are people who don't hesitate to take action and make things happen. Create a predisposition for action by creating specific goals, dividing down work into small chunks, and maintaining forward momentum.
- Create Strong Networks: Surround yourself with supportive mentors, peers, and advisers who can provide advice, feedback, and encouragement. Networking may lead to useful ideas, contacts, and chances for cooperation.

- Stay Focused and Flexible: While it is critical to remain focused on your objectives, you must also be adaptable and open to change your plans. Stay open to new ideas, comments, and market trends, and be ready to change your plan as needed.
- Accept Failure as a Learning Opportunity: Failure is an unavoidable aspect of entrepreneurship, but it can also be a useful instructor. Learn from your mistakes, examine what went wrong, and utilize that information to improve and iterate your strategy.
- Maintain enthusiasm and Purpose: Entrepreneurship may be a difficult and hard path, so it's critical to maintain a strong sense of purpose and enthusiasm for what you do. Allow your enthusiasm to propel you ahead while keeping in mind the effect you want to create with your business.

By adopting these concepts and fostering an entrepreneurial attitude, you will be better prepared to face the challenges and uncertainties of beginning and running a successful firm.

Finding Opportunities for Business Ventures

Identifying chances for business endeavors requires a combination of observation, study, and imagination. Here are some steps that will help you find possible opportunities:

- Observe Market Trends: Be aware of current market trends, growing sectors, and changes in consumer behavior. Pay close attention to changes in technology, legislation, demography, and social values that may provide new possibilities or destabilize established businesses.
- Identify Unmet requirements: Look for market gaps or pain spots where present products or services fall short of meeting consumers' requirements and expectations. Conduct surveys, interviews, and focus groups to better understand consumer pain points and identify areas for innovation and development.
- Follow Your Passions and Expertise: Think of your own interests, hobbies, abilities, and expertise as prospective business chances. Pursuing enterprises that match your passions and talents might boost your drive and resilience as an entrepreneur.
- Explore Niche Markets: Look for underserved or niche markets with minimal competition and high demand. These markets may provide possibilities to cater to certain client segments with distinct requirements or preferences that are not properly met by mainstream products or services.
- Monitor Industry Disruptions: Keep a look out for disruptive technologies, business models, and trends that have the ability to transform sectors and open up new markets. Be proactive in adjusting to change and investigating how you may use these disruptions to your benefit.

- Research rivals: Examine your rivals' strengths, shortcomings, and market positioning to uncover gaps or areas where your goods or services might stand out. Look for ways to provide greater value, superior quality, or unique features that will distinguish you from the competition.
- Consider Franchise or Licensing options: Look into franchise or licensing options that allow you to utilize current brands, processes, and support networks while avoiding some of the risks involved with establishing a new firm from scratch.
- Stay Connected: Use your professional network, which includes colleagues, mentors, industry experts, and alumni groups, to get insights, guidance, and prospective collaborations. Networking may help you find new possibilities and get access to resources and skills that can help you succeed as an entrepreneur.
- Evaluate Emerging Technologies: Stay up to date on technological advancements such as artificial intelligence, blockchain, and biotechnology, which have the potential to generate new markets or disrupt established ones. Investigate how these technologies might be used to address issues or enhance processes across industries.

- Test and confirm Ideas: Once you've found prospective prospects, do market research, prototype development, and pilot programs to measure demand, gather feedback, and confirm your assumptions before investing major resources in a full-scale company.

By taking these actions and keeping open to new ideas, you may improve your chances of discovering profitable business projects and setting yourself for success as an entrepreneur.

Assessing market demand and viability

Assessing market demand and viability is critical to determining whether your company concept has the potential to flourish in the marketplace. To successfully analyze market demand and viability, follow these steps:

- Conduct Market Research: Begin by performing extensive market research to better understand your target audience's needs, tastes, and habits. Gather information on market size, growth patterns, the competitive environment, and consumer demographics to better understand demand for your product or service.

- Identify Your Target Market: Define your target market and segment it according to demographics, psychographics, and geographical location. Understanding your target audience's individual wants, pain spots, and preferences can help you personalize your product and marketing techniques more successfully.
- Evaluate Competitive Landscape: Examine your rivals' products, price, distribution routes, marketing techniques, and strengths and weaknesses. Determine any gaps or places where you might distinguish your product to attract clients and achieve a competitive edge.
- Assess your Unique Value Proposition (UVP): Define your unique value proposition—the specific perks or advantages that distinguish your product or service from rivals and entice buyers. Determine how your UVP meets unmet requirements or solves issues more effectively than existing market options.
- Surveys and Interviews: To confirm your assumptions and evaluate interest in your service, solicit feedback from potential consumers using surveys, interviews, focus groups, or online forums. Ask probing inquiries to learn about their pain spots, preferences, and willingness to pay for your solution.

- Test Minimum Viable Product (MVP): Create a minimum viable product (MVP) or prototype to put your concept to the market and get real-world feedback from early users. Metrics such as client acquisition cost, conversion rate, and retention rate can help you determine the feasibility and scalability of your company strategy.
- Estimate Market Size and Growth: Determine the total addressable market (TAM) for your product or service by calculating the number of prospective consumers and their purchasing power. Consider market growth predictions, trends, and external variables that may influence demand for your product over time.
- Analyze Pricing and Revenue Potential: Determine the best pricing strategy for your product or service based on manufacturing costs, perceived value, rival pricing, and consumer willingness to pay. Calculate prospective income streams and profitability to determine the financial sustainability of your company idea.
- Consider Regulatory and Legal Factors: Look into regulatory restrictions, industry standards, and legal concerns that may affect your capacity to join the market and run your firm. To reduce risks and create consumer trust, ensure compliance with all applicable laws, licenses, permits, and certifications.

By carefully measuring market demand and viability, you can make educated decisions and reduce risks when you start and build your firm. Remember that market research is a continuous process, and staying current on consumer wants and industry trends is critical to long-term success.

CHAPTER TWO
Plan Your Business

Planning your business is an essential step toward establishing the groundwork for success. Here's a thorough approach to efficiently planning your business:

- Define Your Vision and Goals: Begin by establishing your business vision and identifying your long-term objectives. What problem are you trying to solve? What kind of influence do you want to make? Define clear, measurable, attainable, relevant, and time-bound (SMART) objectives to guide your planning process.
- Conduct Market Research: Learn about your target market's demographics, demands, preferences, and purchasing habits. Identify market opportunities and obstacles by analyzing industry trends, the competitive environment, and regulatory needs.
- Create Your Value Proposition: Define your unique value proposition (UVP) – the distinguishing perks or advantages that distinguish your product or service from rivals and attract customers. Explain how your service addresses an issue or meets a demand better than existing options.

- Create a Business Plan: Create a detailed business plan that includes your company's concept, target market, competitive analysis, marketing strategy, operational plan, financial predictions, and growth roadmap. Your business plan acts as a road map for your company and a tool for obtaining capital from investors or lenders.
- Set up Your Business form: Select a legal form for your organization, such as sole proprietorship, partnership, corporation, or limited liability company (LLC). When deciding on the best structure for your firm, consider liability protection, tax ramifications, and administrative needs.
- Register Your Business: Register your company name and receive any licenses, permits, or certificates needed to operate lawfully in your jurisdiction. Investigate local rules and compliance requirements on zoning, health and safety, and industry-specific regulations.
- Secure Financing: Determine the financial resources required to establish and expand your firm, such as starting charges, operational expenditures, and capital investments. Consider financing your company idea with personal savings, loans, grants, investors, or crowdfunding.

- Build Your Team: Determine the core responsibilities and talents needed to run your firm efficiently. Recruit talented people that share your vision and can help to the success of your business. Invest in training and development to create a cohesive, high-performance team.
- Create a marketing strategy that specifies how you intend to recruit, engage, and keep clients. Define your target demographic, messaging, channels, and techniques for attracting and converting prospects to consumers. Allocate resources wisely to maximise the effectiveness of your marketing activities.
- Establish Operational procedures: Create effective and scalable operational procedures to help your business run smoothly and provide a consistent client experience. Create processes, systems, and procedures for product creation, sales, customer support, supply chain management, and other critical aspects of your organization.
- Monitor and adapt: Set key performance indicators (KPIs) to track your company's progress and assess the effectiveness of your plans. Regularly monitor and analyze performance data to discover areas for improvement and make educated decisions about how to adjust and pivot as needed.

Following these steps and putting in the time and effort to design your business will boost your chances of success and provide the groundwork for long-term development and profitability. Remember that planning is an ongoing process, and you must continually examine and adapt your strategy to remain competitive and relevant in an ever-changing business world.

Creating a Solid Business Idea

Creating a strong company concept requires creativity, research, and strategic thought. Here's a step-by-step strategy for developing and refining your company idea:

- Identify Your Passions and Skills: Begin by thinking about your passions, hobbies, and areas of competence. What are you truly enthusiastic about? What talents, expertise, or experiences do you have that may be applied in a business setting? Identifying your abilities and hobbies might help you focus your company idea creation efforts.
- Brainstorm Ideas: Set some time to brainstorm new company ideas. Consider industries, markets, and niches that match your interests and talents. Consider challenges you've faced personally or seen in your community or industry. To develop a diverse set of ideas, use approaches like mind mapping, ideation workshops, or SWOT analysis.

- Research Market Opportunities: Once you've compiled a list of prospective company ideas, undertake market research to determine their viability and demand. Look for market trends, gaps, and opportunities that are relevant to your abilities and interests.
- Validate Your Ideas: Gather input from potential consumers, industry experts, and mentors to determine the feasibility and viability of your company ideas. Surveys, interviews, focus groups, and prototype testing can be used to confirm assumptions, evaluate interest, and uncover possible issues or problems. Pay attention to comments and be willing to refine or pivot your ideas based on the information you receive.
- Define Your Unique Value Proposition (UVP): Clearly describe your company's unique value proposition — the distinguishing perks or advantages that distinguish it from rivals and appeal to your target audience. Determine what makes your product unique, useful, and attractive to customers, and utilize this as the basis for your company plan.
- Consider Scalability and Sustainability: Evaluate your company idea's scalability and long-term viability. Consider aspects like as market size, growth potential, competition hurdles, and operational scalability to see if your concept has the capacity to develop and survive beyond its early phases.

- Financial Viability: Analyze your business idea's revenue potential, cost structure, and profit margins to determine its financial viability. Consider initial costs, operational expenditures, pricing strategies, and revenue sources when determining if your project can create enough cash to be profitable.
- Assess Risk and Mitigation Strategies: Determine the possible risks and obstacles connected with your company plan, such as market competition, regulatory impediments, or technology change. Create mitigation plans to handle these risks and reduce their impact on your organization. Diversification, contingency planning, and risk management methods may help you incorporate resilience into your company model.
- Continuously modify and iterate your company idea in response to feedback, research, and analysis. Be willing to pivot or alter your strategy as needed to better meet market demands, client preferences, and business realities. Adopt an attitude of constant development and adaptation as you create and polish your business concept.

By taking these steps and investing time and effort in establishing a sound business concept, you may improve your chances of success and provide the groundwork for launching and building a profitable firm. Remember that generating a company idea is only the beginning; execution and dedication are essential for making your vision a reality.

Creating a Business Plan

A business plan is vital for setting out your business concept, establishing your strategy, and detailing your path to success. Here's a step-by-step strategy for creating a detailed business plan:

- Begin with an executive summary that describes your business concept, goals, and major plan features. Summarize your unique value offer, target market, revenue model, and growth plan in a succinct and appealing way.
- Business Description: Write a thorough description of your company, including its mission, vision, and goals. Explain the issue or opportunity your company solves, your target market, and the products or services you provide. Explain your company concept, income sources, and competitive advantages.
- Market examination: Conduct an in-depth examination of your target market, including its size, demographics, trends, and development potential. Identify your target clients' requirements, interests, and purchasing habits. Analyze your rivals' strengths, weaknesses, and market position. Highlight possibilities and dangers in the market environment.

- Organization and management: Describe the organizational structure of your company, including essential positions and duties. Introduce your management team, including their backgrounds, expertise, and contributions to the company. Outline any advisory boards, collaborations, or external consultants that assist your company.
- Product or service offerings: Provide specific information about your products or services, such as features, advantages, and price. Highlight your unique selling factors, competitive distinction, and any intellectual property or proprietary technology linked with your product. Discuss your product development strategy and goals for future innovation.
- Marketing and Sales plan: Develop a marketing and sales plan for obtaining and maintaining customers. Define your target market segmentation, positioning, and message. Describe your distribution routes, pricing plan, promotion strategies, and sales projections. Create a timetable for launching marketing efforts and meeting sales objectives.

- Operational Plan: Describe the operational parts of your company, such as manufacturing processes, supply chain management, and logistics. Identify your suppliers, vendors, and partners, and explain how you plan to manage relationships and maintain quality control. Outline your facilities, equipment, technological infrastructure, and any regulatory or compliance needs.
- Financial predictions: Create detailed financial predictions for your company, including income statements, cash flow statements, and balance sheet. Estimate your launch expenditures, ongoing expenses, and revenue expectations over the following three to five years. Support your financial predictions with assumptions, financing sources, and a break-even analysis.
- Risk analysis and contingency planning: Identify any possible risks or uncertainties that may affect your firm, such as market competition, regulatory changes, or economic downturns. Create contingency plans and risk mitigation techniques to manage these issues and reduce their impact on your business operations.
- Appendices: Include any additional information or supporting papers related to your business plan, such as important team members' résumé, market research studies, legal paperwork, or industry certifications. Appendices should be organized in a clear and easy-to-reference fashion.

- Review and Revision: Review your business plan on a regular basis and update it as necessary to reflect changes in your company's environment, market circumstances, or strategic goals. Seek input from mentors, advisers, or industry experts to verify that your strategy stays relevant, reasonable, and in line with your objectives.

By taking these steps and devoting time and effort to developing a complete business plan, you can define your vision, set clear goals, and map a road for building a successful and sustainable organization. A well-written business plan acts as a road map for your entrepreneurial journey and is an effective tool for recruiting investors, partners, and stakeholders to your firm.

Legal Considerations and Registration Processes

Starting a new business necessitates certain legal considerations and registration procedures to guarantee compliance with applicable laws and regulations. Here are some important legal concerns and methods to establish your new business:

- Choose a legal structure. Choosing the right legal form for your company is a critical choice that will impact your responsibility, taxes, and regulatory duties. Common business models include the following:
- Sole Proprietorship: The simplest type of business ownership, with no distinct legal structure; the proprietor is individually accountable for business debts.
- Partnership: Two or more people who share ownership and management duties; partners are personally accountable for business obligations.
- Corporation: A distinct legal entity owned by shareholders; provides limited liability protection to owners but has more complex legal and tax obligations.
- Limited Liability Company (LLC): Combines features of a corporation with a partnership, providing shareholders with limited liability protection and managerial freedom.
- Register your business name. Choose a unique and distinctive name for your company and make sure it is not currently being used by another corporation. Register your business name with the relevant government agency in your area, such as the Secretary of State's office or a local business registration office.

- Obtain Business Licenses and permissions: Look into and obtain any business licenses, permissions, or certificates needed to operate lawfully in your industry and area. The requirements vary according on the sort of business, its location, and industry rules.
- Apply for an Employer Identification Number (EIN): If your company employs workers or is organized as a corporation or partnership, you must receive an Employer Identification Number (EIN) from the Internal Revenue Service. An EIN is required for tax purposes and to create a business bank account.
- Register for Taxes: Determine your federal, state, and local tax responsibilities and register accordingly. Depending on your company's structure and location, this might include income tax, sales tax, payroll tax, or other business taxes.
- Set up Financial Accounts: Create a separate company bank account to keep your business and personal funds separate. This helps to keep accurate financial records, manage business spending, and simplify tax reporting.
- Consider protecting your intellectual property, such as trademarks, copyrights, or patents, to keep your brand, innovations, and creative works from being copied. Consult an intellectual property counsel to evaluate your IP rights and file any appropriate applications for protection.

- Contracts & Agreements: Create the contracts, agreements, and legal papers required for your business operations, such as client contracts, vendor agreements, partnership agreements, and employment contracts. Work with a business attorney to write or review these documents to ensure they protect your interests and follow applicable laws.
- Comply with Regulatory obligations: Understand and follow industry-specific rules, consumer protection laws, employment laws, and other regulatory obligations that may apply to your company. Stay updated about regulatory developments and adapt your rules and procedures accordingly.
- Maintain Corporate documents: Keep correct and current corporate documents, such as meeting minutes, shareholder agreements, and financial statements, as required by law. This helps to establish compliance with legal and regulatory duties while also protecting your company entity's limited liability status.
- Addressing these legal factors and completing the relevant registration processes will help you build a solid legal basis for your new firm and reduce the chance of future legal or compliance difficulties. Consider talking with legal and financial specialists to verify that you are in compliance with all applicable rules and regulations while also successfully protecting your company interests.

CHAPTER THREE
Executing Your Business Idea

Executing your company concept entails putting your vision into reality and establishing a solid basis for your venture. Here's a step-by-step approach to assist you properly implement your company concept.

- Create a Detailed Business Plan: If you haven't already, write a complete business plan outlining your objectives, target market, competition analysis, marketing strategy, operational plan, financial forecasts, and growth strategy. Your business plan acts as a road map for your company, offering a framework for decision-making and resource allocation.
- Secure Funding: Determine the financial resources required to start and build your firm, and look into funding opportunities including personal savings, loans, grants, investors, or crowdsourcing. Create a financial strategy outlining your starting costs, running expenditures, income predictions, and capital needs.

- Set up your infrastructure. Establish the infrastructure and resources required to run your firm, such as physical premises, equipment, technological systems, and legal and administrative procedures. Make sure you have the right tools and procedures in place to help your business run smoothly.
- Build Your Team: Recruit and onboard outstanding employees that share your vision and can contribute to the success of your company. Define roles and duties, provide clear communication routes, and cultivate a collaborative and supportive workplace culture. Invest in training and development to empower your employees and improve their skills and talents.
- Develop Your Product or Service: If you have a product or service, focus on developing and refining it to fulfill client demands and provide value. Conduct market research, collect consumer feedback, and iterate on your product or service based on your findings and learnings. Make sure your product is high-quality, dependable, and consistent with your brand promise.

- Implement Your Marketing Strategy: Follow your marketing plan to acquire, engage, and retain consumers. Use a combination of online and offline marketing channels, such as digital marketing, social media, content marketing, email marketing, advertising, events, and networking, to reach your target demographic and increase brand recognition. Monitor the effectiveness of your marketing activities and alter your plans based on the results.
- Launch Your Business: To build buzz and attract clients, start with a powerful marketing strategy and promotional events. Consider holding a launch event, giving special specials or discounts, and utilizing social media and public relations channels to spread the news about your company. Ensure that you provide a consistent and favorable client experience from the moment you debut.
- Manage Operations and Finances: Implement effective operational procedures and systems to manage day-to-day activities, simplify workflows, and maximize resource usage. Monitor your finances attentively, check spending and sales, and properly manage cash flow to maintain your company's financial health and sustainability.

- Adapt and innovate: Maintain agility and responsiveness to changes in the market, client preferences, and industry trends. Continuously monitor performance indicators, get feedback, and iterate on your plans to enhance and evolve your services. Adopt a culture of experimentation, learning, and adaptability to remain ahead of the competition and achieve long-term success.

By taking these steps and implementing your company concept with purpose and drive, you may boost your chances of creating a successful and long-lasting firm. Remember that execution is essential for making your idea a reality, so be focused, adaptable, and devoted to your goals as you navigate the obstacles and possibilities of entrepreneurship.